NAT
TURNER

and the
Slave Revolt

by Tracy Barrett

GATEWAY CIVIL RIGHTS
THE MILLBROOK PRESS
BROOKFIELD, CONNECTICUT

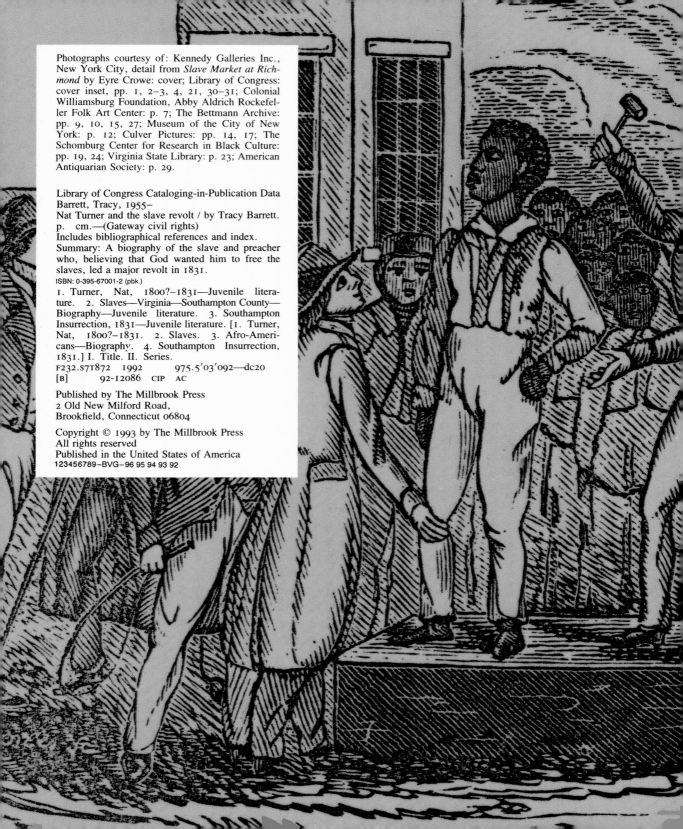

Photographs courtesy of: Kennedy Galleries Inc., New York City, detail from *Slave Market at Richmond* by Eyre Crowe: cover; Library of Congress: cover inset, pp. 1, 2–3, 4, 21, 30–31; Colonial Williamsburg Foundation, Abby Aldrich Rockefeller Folk Art Center: p. 7; The Bettmann Archive: pp. 9, 10, 15, 27; Museum of the City of New York: p. 12; Culver Pictures: pp. 14, 17; The Schomburg Center for Research in Black Culture: pp. 19, 24; Virginia State Library: p. 23; American Antiquarian Society: p. 29.

Library of Congress Cataloging-in-Publication Data
Barrett, Tracy, 1955–
Nat Turner and the slave revolt / by Tracy Barrett.
p.   cm.—(Gateway civil rights)
Includes bibliographical references and index.
Summary: A biography of the slave and preacher who, believing that God wanted him to free the slaves, led a major revolt in 1831.
ISBN: 0-395-67001-2 (pbk.)
1. Turner, Nat, 1800?–1831—Juvenile literature. 2. Slaves—Virginia—Southampton County—Biography—Juvenile literature. 3. Southampton Insurrection, 1831—Juvenile literature. [1. Turner, Nat, 1800?–1831. 2. Slaves. 3. Afro-Americans—Biography. 4. Southampton Insurrection, 1831.] I. Title. II. Series.
F232.S7T872   1992   975.5'03'092—dc20
[B]   92-12086   CIP   AC

Published by The Millbrook Press
2 Old New Milford Road,
Brookfield, Connecticut 06804

THE

CONFESSIONS

OF

NAT TURNER,

THE LEADER

OF

THE LATE INSURRECTION

IN SOUTHAMPTON, VA.

AS FULLY AND VOLUNTARILY MADE TO

THOMAS R. GRAY,

In the prison where he was confined, and acknowledged by him to be such,
when read before the Court of Southampton: with the
certificate, under seal of the Court convened at
Jerusalem, Nov. 5, 1831, for his trial.

ALSO,

AN AUTHENTIC ACCOUNT

OF THE

WHOLE INSURRECTION,

WITH

Lists of the Whites who were Murdered,

AND OF THE

*Negroes brought before the Court of Southampton,
and there sentenced, &c.*

———

RICHMOND:

PUBLISHED BY THOMAS R. GRAY.

T. W. WHITE, PRINTER.

....

1832.

On *November 5, 1831,* Nat Turner was taken in chains from a jail cell to the Southampton County Courthouse, in Hampton County, Virginia. Deputies held back the huge, angry crowd that threatened to lynch the prisoner on his way to trial.

In the courtroom, Turner, a thirty-one-year-old man with a broad face and large, piercing eyes, stood calmly while a clerk read the charges: "Nat, alias Nat Turner, a negro slave . . . charged with conspiring to rebel and making insurrection."

His accusers said that he was the leader of a gang that had murdered from fifty-five to sixty people—women, men, children, and even babies. Turner replied that he did not feel at all guilty. He and the other slaves who had joined in his rebellion had killed those people, he said, but the victims deserved to die. They were slave owners.

The trial was over in a matter of minutes. The judge told Turner, "The judgment of the Court is, that you be taken hence to the jail from whence you came, thence to the place of execution, and on Friday next, between the hours of 10 A.M. and 2 P.M., be hung by the neck until you are dead! dead! dead! and may the Lord have mercy upon your soul."

Less than a week later, Turner was hung. In the days between his sentencing and his hanging, he told his story to a lawyer named Thomas R. Gray, who published these conversations in a pamphlet called *The Confessions of Nat Turner.*

The story of Nat Turner and his slave revolt spread throughout the nation. To many people he was a hero, a man who had died with courage rather than live his life in chains. To others he was a madman and a murderer. In either case, Turner's rebellion made people aware of the evil of slavery and so helped to bring about its end.

Marked at Birth

Nat Turner was born on October 2, 1800, on a farm in Southampton County, Virginia. His mother had come to the United States only three years before his birth. She had been born in Africa and lived there until she was a teenager, when slave traders kidnapped her along with many other Africans. She was brought on a boat across the Atlantic Ocean to the port of Norfolk, Virginia, on the southern tip of the Chesapeake Bay. There she was sold into slavery.

A farmer named Benjamin Turner bought her. Slave owners did not like their slaves to keep their African names, so they often gave them their own family name. Nat's mother came to be known as Nancy Turner.

Nat's father was a slave born in the United States. But Nat did not know his father very well, because when Nat was just

The enslavement of blacks in the American Colonies began
in the 1600s and continued to flourish until the Civil War
in 1861. By that time, nearly four million people, nearly
a third of the South's population, were slaves.

a child, his father ran away. No one knows if he made it to freedom or if he died on the way, because no one, including Nat and Nancy, ever heard from him again.

Nat was raised by his mother and his grandmother (his father's mother). When he was born, he had some strange bumps and marks on his skin. In the part of Africa where his mother came from, these marks were thought to mean that Nat would grow up to be a great religious leader. So Nancy and her friends watched him eagerly to see if he would do anything unusual.

One day when Nat was just three or four years old, his mother heard him talking to his friends about something that had happened before he was born. She told him that he couldn't possibly know about it, because he wasn't even alive at the time. He insisted that he did know, and to prove it he told her many details about the incident. She called her friends over, and they all listened in amazement as he told them about things that had happened years before.

Perhaps Nat had simply overheard his parents and their friends talking about these things. But people believed that he had a special, magical connection with God. Then he did something else that made him stand out. In those days, not many people, especially slaves, knew how to read and write. Nat's mother was among those who could not. There were no schools for slave children, and many slave owners were careful to make sure that their slaves didn't learn to read and write for fear the slaves would write letters to each other and help each other escape or fight their owners. But somehow, Nat learned how to read by himself.

The slave owners had good reason to be afraid that their slaves might learn to read. If slaves could read newspapers, they might find out that other slaves were fighting their owners and, in some cases, killing them, in order to be free. Less than ten years before Nat Turner was born, the slaves on the island of Santo Domingo, near Cuba, had risen up against their owners and won their freedom, after 60,000 people, both black and white, had died. The former slaves set up a new government and established the country of Haiti—the first country in the Western Hemisphere to be ruled by black people.

Toussaint-L'Ouverture, a former slave, led the successful revolt of the black population on French-ruled Santo Domingo in 1791.

In 1799, the year before Nat was born, some slaves near the Turner farm killed two white people in an attempt to escape. They were caught and put to death. One year later, in 1800, some free blacks in Richmond, Virginia, read about the American and French revolutions and were inspired by their ideals of equality for all. They were planning a rebellion against the whites of the city when they were caught. Although they had not yet harmed anyone, the leader and thirty-four of his followers were hung.

Since Nat was just a child, though, Benjamin Turner had as yet no reason to fear that he might read of these events and decide to do something similar. He was proud of Nat and even showed him off to his friends. Benjamin took him to Bible meetings, where Nat listened eagerly to stories from the Bible.

This picture exaggerates the free form of worship in black prayer meetings.

He was even given a Bible of his own, which he used to read to himself and, later, to the other slaves.

Slaveholders encouraged their slaves to be Christians. They also found passages in the Bible that they felt supported their belief that God wanted them to have slaves and that it was all right to beat slaves when they didn't obey. One line they especially wanted their slaves to hear was, "For he who knoweth his Master's will, and doeth it not, shall be beaten with many stripes, and thus have I chastened [punished] you."

But Nat was learning things from the Bible that Benjamin Turner never intended. No one knows exactly what he read, but it is likely that the Old Testament and its stories of the prophets and the revolts by the enslaved Jews caught his attention.

"Seek Ye the Kingdom of Heaven"

Meanwhile, times were getting hard in Virginia. Most slave ships unloaded their human cargo in ports along the Virginia coast. Buyers would come from other states to find new slaves to take home. But when these states fell into economic hard times, people stopped buying slaves. As a result, Virginia grew poorer, too.

Field hands put in long, hard hours in cotton fields during the harvest.

Benjamin Turner's son Samuel could not afford to buy his own slaves, so his father loaned him Nat, who was then nine years old, and Nat's mother. When Nat turned twelve, his new owner decided that he was old enough to work in the fields.

Working in the fields was hard and boring. Nat had seen other slaves doing this work, but he had always thought he was special—after all, he had been born with his marks. But now here he was, doing backbreaking work in the burning-hot fields six days a week from sunup to sundown.

One day at a prayer meeting, Nat heard a black preacher recite a line from the Bible: ''Seek ye the kingdom of Heaven and all things shall be added to you.'' A few weeks later, while working in the fields, Nat suddenly thought he heard a voice in the wind. He stopped working to listen more carefully. The voice repeated the words of the preacher: ''Seek ye the kingdom of Heaven and all things shall be added to you.'' A few weeks later, he heard the voice again. Nat thought that this was God talking to him, telling him that if he did what was asked, he would become a famous leader. He tried to please God: He didn't drink alcohol; he didn't smoke; and even if he had the chance, he never stole anything. He got married, too. His wife, Cherry, was also a slave.

Samuel Turner kept making Nat work in the fields, though, and even worse, he decided that his slaves were not working hard enough. In 1821 he hired a new overseer to push the slaves to work harder. Perhaps remembering his father's example, Turner ran away, leaving his mother and Cherry behind.

Nat Turner was a valuable slave, and Samuel must have sent people to look for him and advertised in the newspapers for his return. But when Turner had not been caught after a month, Samuel must have been close to giving up.

A dog has picked up the scent of the runaway slave, and the overseer is not far behind.

So imagine everyone's surprise when, exactly thirty days after he had escaped, Nat Turner showed up on Samuel Turner's doorstep. No one had found him; he had decided to come back on his own. The other slaves told him he was crazy. Why had he chosen to return to a life of slavery? Turner answered, ''The Spirit appeared to me and said I had my wishes directed to the things of this world, and not to the kingdom of heaven, and that I should return to the service of my earthly master.'' And then he added, ''For he who knoweth his Master's will, and doeth it not, shall be beaten with many stripes, and thus have I chastened you.'' This angered and puzzled the other slaves. Why should the man they looked up to quote the very line that the slave owners used against them? What they didn't know was that Nat Turner had a plan. He would punish the slave owners just as they had punished the slaves for so many years.

$200

REWARD!

Ran away from his owner [a Lady residing near Upper Marlboro, Prince George's County, Md.] on r about th   t Mulla-
to man na   he is
bout five   ey eyes,
low in sp   earance,
bout twen   od.

One Hu   ehended
vithin thir   irty, the
bove rewa   so that
is owner'

THE DREAM OF FREEDOM

Some people said that it was not as bad to be a slave in the upper southern states of Virginia and Maryland as it was in the Deep South. But Nat Turner and his vision of rebellion came from Virginia. Frederick Douglass and Harriet Tubman, two heroic people who worked all their lives to free the slaves, were born in nearby Maryland.

It was true that slaves in the states of Maryland and Virginia were often treated better than those on the plantations in Alabama, Mississippi, Georgia, and Louisiana. But no matter what the circumstances, when a person was treated like the property of another person, life was hopeless and cruel.

Perhaps life for a slave in nineteenth-century America so close to the border between North and South only made the dream of freedom all the stronger. Those who fought it paved the way for the Civil War, which in 1865 finally brought the system of slavery to an end.

for the owner,

Buena Vista Post Office, Prince George's Co. Md.

He did not have to wait long. On May 12, 1828, Turner received his clearest vision. He later described it: "I heard a loud noise in the heavens, and the Spirit instantly appeared to me and said the Serpent was loosened, and Christ had laid down the yoke he had borne for the sins of men, and that I should take it on and fight against the Serpent." Turner thought that the serpent represented slavery. The spirit went on to say that he would receive another sign when it was time to take up the work that Christ had begun.

Turner must have grown impatient as the years passed and still he waited for the promised sign. Then, in February of 1831, an eclipse of the sun darkened the entire sky. Nat Turner, who like all slaves was unschooled in the laws of the universe, had no way of knowing that an eclipse was a perfectly natural event. He saw it as the sign that the spirit had promised him.

"The Great Day of Judgment"

Nat Turner chose four fellow slaves—Henry Porter, Hark Travis, Nelson Williams, and Sam Francis—to help him get ready for battle. First they planned to start their rebellion on the Fourth of July, the day that the Declaration of Independence was signed. But Turner was sick at the time. After he recovered, the five

In a secret meeting, Nat Turner shares his vision of freedom with a group of fellow slaves. He believed that the heavens were behind him. It was time to revolt.

men decided to create a plan to put into action as soon as they received one more sign. Later, another slave named Will appeared at one of their meetings. Turner was suspicious of him at first. But when the newcomer said that if he couldn't be free, he would just as soon be dead, Turner and his friends knew that he could be trusted.

In August, the sky was once again filled with mystery. When the sun rose, it looked green, and then it turned a strange shade of blue. Then a dark spot moved across its surface. People all over the eastern part of the United States, not just in Virginia, were terrified by this fantastic sight. But Nat and his followers were convinced that this was the sign they were waiting for. "Just as the black spot passed over the sun, so shall the blacks pass over the earth," Turner told them.

They decided to begin their battle on Sunday night. They planned to kill every white person in the area, old or young, male or female. So on Sunday, August 22, the bloody fighting began. The rebels decided that Nat Turner, their leader, should kill the first victim.

When the Travises, for whom Nat had worked for several years, were asleep in their beds, Turner and his followers let themselves into their house and killed them all, including two children and a baby. Turner and his followers then ran down the lane and killed Salanthiel Francis in his nearby farm. The next house they came to belonged to a Mrs. Reese, whom they killed in her sleep. Her son woke up, but, as Turner said later, "it was only to sleep the sleep of death, he had only time to say who is that, and he was no more."

As they went, they picked up swords, guns, shovels—anything they could find that would help them. They went from house to house, killing every white person they came upon, slave owner or not, man or woman, adult or child, kind or cruel. They didn't use the guns they had found yet, for fear that someone would hear them and find out what they were doing in time to warn the rest of the white people.

This woodcut tells the story of Turner's rebellion in scenes 1 through 4. A mother tries to protect her children; a white man is killed; another defends himself; and, finally, soldiers on horseback ride after the rebels who flee for their lives.

Some of the slaves in the houses they came to joined them; others ran away in terror. For a long time, no one knew what was going on. Turner's gang killed every white person they saw, and the slaves had no way of spreading the word that Nat Turner and a group of men were on their way, intending to kill every white person in Southampton County.

It was a long time before Turner killed anyone himself. He had struck at Joseph Travis, and he had wounded a woman named Mrs. Newsome. But then they came to the house of a preacher and his wife; Richard and Caty Whitehead. Will killed them both. Their daughter Margaret was trying to escape, but Turner ran after her and hit her again and again with his ax until she, too, was dead. Another daughter, Harriet, was saved by Hubbard, one of the Whiteheads' slaves, who hid her under a mat in her room and told the rebels that no one was in there. After the rebels left, and Hubbard went out of the house to see exactly what had happened, Harriet ran out into the woods and hid until some white men found her the next day.

The bloody work continued all morning and into the afternoon. Family after family was killed. Only a few escaped. In one case, a woman hid under a mattress while her sister was murdered in the same room with her. When Turner and his followers came to a school, they killed all eleven people they found there: the teacher and ten children.

When the children saw the rebels approaching, a twelve-year-old girl named Clarinda Jones hid from them outside the schoolhouse. She then ran as fast as she could to the woods.

One of the rebels saw her and shot at her, wounding her slightly. She fell flat in the tall grass where no one could see her. After the killers left, she ran into a nearby swamp and spent the night there. The next day she was taken home to her mother and father, who asked her how she, of all the children, had managed to escape. She told them, "The Lord helped me."

The house of Major Thomas Ridley was a safe place where whites could hide.

The First War

With no telephones, no radio, and no television to let people know what was happening, no cars to drive away in, and no police to run to, the white people were unable to get help. Turner's gang met with little resistance for hours. But some of the slaves who had refused to join in managed to spread the word that something dreadful was happening. A schoolteacher, after coming home to find his wife and child dead, rode on his

HARRIET TUBMAN

Harriet Tubman was born into slavery around 1820. When she was a girl in Dorchester County, Maryland, a slave owner threw a lead weight at another slave who was trying to escape. The weight hit Harriet on the forehead. This huge blow caused her to suffer for the rest of her life from a disorder that made her fall asleep without warning several times a day.

When Harriet Tubman got older, she left her parents, her brothers and sisters, and her husband behind to escape to freedom in Philadelphia, Pennsylvania. After a few years, she began making trips to the South to lead her fellow people from captivity to the Promised Land of the North. She followed a carefully planned route under cover of darkness, stopping along the way at the homes of people who were against slavery. This secret roadway was known as the Underground Railroad.

Harriet Tubman heard of Nat Turner's slave revolt when she was a girl. His violent rebellion both inspired and frightened her.

In some ways, Harriet Tubman was like Nat Turner. She, like Turner, refused to live in slavery. Like Turner, too, her own personal freedom was not as important to her as the freedom of all slaves. And like Nat Turner, Harriet Tubman thought that God spoke to her to tell her how to help others. But she worked in a much different way.

fastest horse to Murfreesboro, North Carolina, where the cavalry was stationed. By Monday afternoon, a group of armed white men was gathering to protect those white people who were left.

Now the killings turned into a battle. The blacks were not as well armed as the whites, since the few guns they had were meant for hunting, not fighting. Besides, the slaves were untrained at war, while white people were soon joined by well-trained soldiers from North Carolina. The slaves were now fighting for their lives. The two sides met at Parker's Field, where they clashed in a savage battle. In the end every rebel was either killed or captured, except a few who fled for their lives. Among the runaways was Nat Turner.

Just as Turner and his followers had determined to kill every white person they met, many of the white people coming to join the fight decided to kill every black person they met. Some were terrified that the blacks would kill all the whites, but some just used this fear as an excuse to commit murder. Some blacks who weren't even aware of what was happening were killed by gangs of whites. The cavalry from Murfreesboro, which was supposed to be well trained and to know how to handle an emergency, rode through the area and killed forty or more blacks. Some of these people might have been involved in the rebellion, but many of them certainly were not.

Where was Nat Turner while all this was happening? He knew that his rebellion had failed, and he knew that people were looking for him. He said later, "After having supplied myself with provisions from Mr. Travis's, I scratched a hole under a pile of fence rails in a field, where I concealed myself for six weeks, never leaving my hiding place but for a few minutes in the dead of night to get water." But he knew that sooner or later he would be found. And sure enough, one day, by accident, a hunting dog led his two black masters to Turner. He begged them not to tell anyone where he was, but they told some white people, who came looking for him. He was finally captured on Sunday, October 30.

Nat Turner's trial was swift, but by the time he was hanged, everyone in the country knew his name and the story—often greatly exaggerated—about how he had led the slaves of Southampton County to revolt.

The effects of his rebellion have been hard to pin down. Some white people, especially abolitionists, people who were actively against slavery, saw the rebellion as proof that slavery must be abolished, or ended. They pointed to Nat Turner and his followers as examples. They had not been treated as badly as some slaves, but they still hated their lives so much that they would rather die than remain slaves. If even the best form of slavery was that bad, all slavery must be done away with.

Turner went into hiding after his August 22 revolt, but on October 30 he was caught.

Yet other white people, especially slave owners, insisted that the problem was not with slavery itself, but with the way Turner and his followers were allowed to get ideas. If Nat had not learned how to read and if slaves had not been allowed the freedom to meet each other without a white person being present, they would never have gotten the idea that slaves should be freed.

So these people made new, stricter laws, aimed at keeping even tighter controls on the slaves. But the effect of these laws was the opposite of what the lawmakers wanted: The slaves grew even angrier, and the abolitionists saw the laws as yet another example of the slave owners' cruelty. It is possible that these laws, which were meant to keep slavery around longer, actually helped shorten its life.

But nothing could erase the fact that hundreds of people had died in those few days in 1831. No one knows for certain, but about sixty whites and as many as two hundred blacks lost their lives. Many of the whites killed were children, and some were poor farmers who had no slaves. Most of the blacks killed had had nothing to do with the rebellion.

Nat Turner's rebellion later came to be called the first war against slavery; the Civil War was called the second. His revolt, bloody and violent as it was, helped to inspire the brave people who finally brought an end to slavery in the United States.

The story of the Nat Turner rebellion in the Liberator, *1831.*

IMPORTANT DATES IN THE LIFE OF NAT TURNER

1800   Nat Turner is born on October 2 in Southampton County, Virginia.

1821   Turner runs away from his owner, Samuel Turner. Thirty days later he returns of his own free will.

1828   On May 12 Turner has a vision that he thinks comes from God.

1831   In February Turner interprets an eclipse as the promised sign.

In early August he sees another sign in the form of an eclipse.

On August 22 he leads a group of fellow slaves to revolt.

On October 20 Turner is caught.

On November 5 Turner is tried and convicted of murder.

On November 11, 1831, Nat Turner is executed.

FIND OUT MORE ABOUT NAT TURNER AND HIS TIMES

Escape from Slavery: Five Journeys to Freedom by Doreen Rappaport (New York: HarperCollins, 1991).

Harriet Tubman and the Underground Railroad by Dan Elish (Brookfield, Conn.: The Millbrook Press, 1993).

Nat Turner by Terry Bisson (New York: Chelsea House, 1988).

Nat Turner by Judith Berry Griffin (New York: Coward; McCann & Geoghegan, 1970).

Out of the Mouths of Slaves by Carole Marsh (Decatur, Ga.: Gallopade Publishing Group, 1989).

A young slave family tries to run to freedom.

INDEX

Page numbers in *italics* refer to illustrations.